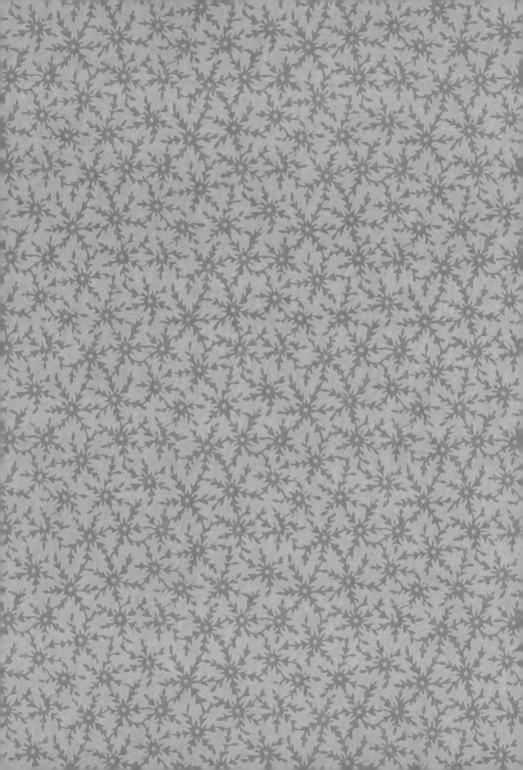

Amazing Grace

Ellie Claire
gift & paper expressions

...inspired by life

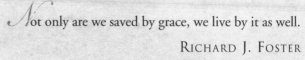

Not only are we saved by grace, we live by it as well.

RICHARD J. FOSTER

*From the fullness of His grace we have all received one blessing
after another.*

JOHN 1:16 NIV

The most glorious promises of God are generally fulfilled in such a wondrous manner that He steps forth to save us at a time when there is the least appearance of it.

KARL HEINRICH VON BOGATZKY

As for God, His way is perfect. The word of the Lord is proven; He is a shield to all who trust in Him.

2 SAMUEL 22:31 NKJV

*W*e don't have to be perfect.... We are asked only to be
real, trusting in His perfection to cover our imperfection,
knowing that one day we will finally be all that
Christ saved us for and wants us to be.

GIGI GRAHAM TCHIVIDJIAN

*W*hen perfection comes, the things that are not perfect will
end.... Now we see a dim reflection...but then we shall see
clearly. Now I know only a part, but then I will know fully,
as God has known me.

1 CORINTHIANS 13:9, 12 NCV

Amazing Grace (How sweet the sound)
That saved a wretch like me!...

Amazing Grace (How sweet the sound)
That saved a wretch like me!...

There is no one so far lost that Jesus cannot find
him and cannot save him.

ANDREW MURRAY

When they cried out to You again, You heard from heaven.
Because of Your mercy, You saved them again and again.

NEHEMIAH 9:28 NCV

Grace and gratitude belong together like heaven and earth. Grace evokes gratitude like the voice an echo. Gratitude follows grace as thunder follows lightning.

KARL BARTH

I give thanks to God with everything I've got.... God's works are so great, worth a lifetime of study—endless enjoyment!... His generosity never gives out.... He's so personal and holy, worthy of our respect.

PSALM 111:1-3, 10 THE MESSAGE

Amazing Grace (How sweet the sound)
That saved a wretch like me!...

Amazing Grace (How sweet the sound)
That saved a wretch like me!...

Grace is something you can never get but can only be given. There's no way to earn it or deserve it.... A good night sleep is grace and so are good dreams. Most tears are grace.... Somebody loving you is grace.

FREDERICK BUECHNER

Surely Your goodness and love will be with me all my life, and I will live in the house of the Lord forever.

PSALM 23:6 NCV

Amazing Grace
(How sweet the sound)
That saved a wretch like me!
I once was lost,
but now am found,
Was blind, but now I see.

I once was lost, but now am found,
Was blind, but now I see....

The "air" which our souls need also envelops all of us at all times and on all sides. God is round about us in Christ on every hand, with many-sided and all-sufficient grace. All we need to do is to open our hearts.

OLE HALLESBY

But God had special plans for me and set me apart for His work even before I was born. He called me through His grace.

GALATIANS 1:15 NCV

God wishes to be seen, and He wishes to be sought, and
He wishes to be expected, and He wishes to be trusted.

JULIAN OF NORWICH

You will seek Me and find Me when you seek Me
with all your heart.

JEREMIAH 29:13 NIV

I once was lost, but now am found,
Was blind, but now, I see . . . .

I once was lost, but now am found,
Was blind, but now I see....

God is looking for people who will come in simple dependence upon His grace, and rest in simple faith upon His greatness. At this very moment, He's looking at you.

JACK HAYFORD

Depend on the Lord; trust Him, and He will take care of you.

PSALM 37:5 NLT

I am not what I ought to be, I am not what I wish to be, I am not what I hope to be; but, by the grace of God, I am not what I was.

JOHN NEWTON

For we are God's masterpiece. He has created us anew in Christ Jesus, so we can do the good things He planned for us long ago.

EPHESIANS 2:10 NLT

I once was lost, but now am found,
Was blind, but now I see....

I once was lost, but now am found,
Was blind, but now I see. . . .

Faith in God is not blind. It is based on
His character and His promises.

Take on an entirely new way of life—a God-fashioned
life, a life renewed from the inside and working itself
into your conduct as God accurately reproduces
His character in you.

EPHESIANS 4:24 THE MESSAGE

Christ knew His Father and offered Himself unreservedly into His hands. If we let ourselves be lost for His sake, trusting the same God as Lord of all, we shall find safety where Christ found His, in the bosom of the Father.

ELISABETH ELLIOT

Those who live in the shelter of the Most High will find rest in the shadow of the Almighty.

PSALM 91:1 NLT

I once was lost, but now am found,
Was blind but now I see. . . .

I once was lost, but now am found,
Was blind, but now I see....

I know, more surely than I know anything, that any pang of healing or forgiveness or goodness I have ever felt comes solely from the grace of God.

PHILIP YANCEY

Grace, because God is putting everything together again through the Messiah, invites us into life—a life that goes on and on and on, world without end.

ROMANS 5:21 THE MESSAGE

'Twas grace that taught
my heart to fear,
And grace my fears relieved;
How precious did
that grace appear,
The hour I first believed!

'Twas grace that taught my heart to fear,
And grace my fears relieved. . . .

*D*on't we all long for a father...who cares for us in spite of our failures? We do have that type of a father. A father who is at His best when we are at our worst...whose grace is strongest when our devotion is weakest.

MAX LUCADO

*T*his is your Father you are dealing with, and He knows better than you what you need. With a God like this loving you, you can pray very simply.

MATTHEW 6:7 THE MESSAGE

The beauty of grace—our only permanent deliverance from guilt—is that it meets us where we are and gives us what we don't deserve.

CHARLES R. SWINDOLL

For by grace you have been saved through faith, and that not of yourselves; it is the gift of God, not of works, lest anyone should boast.

EPHESIANS 2:8-9 NKJV

'Twas grace that taught my heart to fear,
And grace my fears relieved. . . .

'Twas grace that taught my heart to fear,
And grace my fears relieved. . . .

*C*ome, Thou long-expected Jesus,
born to set Thy people free;
From our fears and sins release us;
let us find our rest in Thee.

CHARLES WESLEY

*R*est in the Lord, and wait patiently for Him.

PSALM 37:7 NKJV

We sometimes fear to bring our troubles to God, because they must seem so small to Him who sitteth on the circle of the earth. But if they are large enough to vex and endanger our welfare, they are large enough to touch His heart of love.

REUBEN A. TORREY

Cast your worries to the Lord, and He will take care of you.
He will never let the good people down.

PSALM 55:22 NCV

'Twas grace that taught my heart to fear,
And grace my fears relieved. . . .

'Twas grace that taught my heart to fear,
And grace my fears relieved. . . .

I trust You always though I may seem to be lost and in the shadow of death. I will not fear, for You are ever with me. And You will never leave me to face my perils alone.

THOMAS MERTON

Yea, though I walk through the valley of the shadow of death, I will fear no evil; for You are with me; Your rod and Your staff, they comfort me.

PSALM 23:4 NKJV

It is only with the help of His grace that we are able to persevere in spiritual contemplation with endless wonder at His high, surpassing, immeasurable love which our Lord in His goodness has for us.

JULIAN OF NORWICH

Blessed is the man who perseveres under trial, because when he has stood the test, he will receive the crown of life that God has promised to those who love Him.

JAMES 1:12 NIV

'Twas grace that taught my heart to fear.
And grace my fears relieved. . . .

'Twas grace that taught my heart to fear,
And grace my fears relieved. . . .

*G*od Incarnate is the end of fear; and the heart
that realizes that He is in the midst, that takes heed
to the assurance of His loving presence,
will be quiet in the midst of alarm.

F. B. MEYER

*I*n peace I will lie down and sleep, for You alone, O Lord,
will keep me safe.

PSALM 4:8 NLT

'Twas grace that taught
my heart to fear,
And grace my fears relieved:
How precious did
that grace appear,
The hour I first believed!

How precious did that grace appear,
The hour I first believed!....

Have confidence in God's mercy, for when you think He
is a long way from you, He is often quite near.

THOMAS À KEMPIS

God saved us from these great dangers of death, and He will
continue to save us. We have put our hope in Him,
and He will save us again.

2 CORINTHIANS 1:10 NCV

Look deep within yourself and recognize what brings life and grace into your heart. It is this that can be shared with those around you. You are loved by God. This is an inspiration to love.

CHRISTOPHER DE VINCK

It is clear to us, friends, that God not only loves you very much but also has put His hand on you for something special. When the Message we preached came to you, it wasn't just words. Something happened in you.

1 THESSALONIANS 1:4-5 THE MESSAGE

How precious did that grace appear,
The hour I first believed! . . . .

How precious did that grace appear,
The hour I first believed!...

The grace is God's: the faith is ours. God gave us the free will with which to choose. God gave us the capacity to believe and trust.

BILLY GRAHAM

God is able to make all grace abound to you, so that in all things at all times, having all that you need, you will abound in every good work.

2 CORINTHIANS 9:8 NIV

The Lord's chief desire is to reveal Himself to you and, in order for Him to do that, He gives you abundant grace.... He touches you, and His touch is so delightful that, more than ever, you are drawn inwardly to Him.

MADAME JEANNE GUYON

The Lord is near to all who call upon Him,
to all who call upon Him in truth.

PSALM 145:18 NKJV

How precious did that grace appear,
The hour I first believed!...

How precious did that grace appear,
The hour I first believed!....

God delights to meet the faith of one who looks up to
Him and says, "Lord, You know that I cannot do this—
but I believe that You can!"

AMY CARMICHAEL

*Depend on the Lord and His strength; always go to Him for
help. Remember the miracles He has done;
remember His wonders.*

PSALM 105:4-5 NCV

At the very heart and foundation of all God's dealings with us,...we must dare to believe in and assert the infinite, unmerited, and unchanging love of God.

L. B. COWMAN

I trust in Your unfailing love. I will rejoice because You have rescued me.

PSALM 13:5 NLT

How precious did that grace appear,
The hour I first believed!....

How precious did that grace appear,
The hour I first believed!....

How could I be anything but quite happy if I believed always that all the past is forgiven, and all the present furnished with power, and all the future bright with hope.

JAMES SMETHAM

His compassions never fail. They are new every morning; great is Your faithfulness.

LAMENTATIONS 3:22-23 NIV

Thro' many dangers,
toils and snare,
I have already come;
'Tis grace has brought me
safe thus far,
And grace will
lead me home.

Thro' many dangers, toils and snare,
I have already come....

Grace may be unnoticed. But there are usually some who will notice... [They] will notice even its lightest touch, and will hold it a precious, and incalculably valuable thing.

ELISABETH ELLIOT

But by the grace of God I am what I am, and His grace to me was not without effect. No, I worked harder than all of them—yet not I, but the grace of God that was with me.

1 CORINTHIANS 15:10 NIV

God has not promised sun without rain, joy without sorrow, peace without pain.
But God has promised strength for the day, rest for the labor, light for the way,
grace for the trials, help from above, unfailing sympathy, undying love.

ANNIE JOHNSON FLINT

Let the beloved of the Lord rest secure in Him, for He shields
him all day long, and the one the Lord loves rests
between His shoulders.

DEUTERONOMY 33:12 NIV

Thro' many dangers, toils and snare,
I have already come.....

Thro' many dangers, toils and snare,
I have already come. . . .

We know that [God] gives us every grace,
every abundant grace; and though we are so weak of
ourselves, this grace is able to carry us through
every obstacle and difficulty.

ELIZABETH ANN SETON

Let us hold tightly without wavering to the hope we affirm,
for God can be trusted to keep His promise.

HEBREWS 10:23 NLT

When we focus on God, the scene changes. He's in control of our lives; nothing lies outside the realm of His redemptive grace. Even when we make mistakes, fail in relationships, or deliberately make bad choices, God can redeem us.

PENELOPE J. STOKES

The Lord will work out His plans for my life—for Your faithful love, O Lord, endures forever.

PSALM 138:8 NLT

....

....

....

....

....

....

....

....

....

....

....

Thro' many dangers, toils and snare,
I have already come.....

Thro' many dangers, toils and snare,
I have already come. . . .

God will lift up all who have a humble spirit and save
them in all trials and tribulations.

THOMAS À KEMPIS

The Lord is good, a strong refuge when trouble comes.
He is close to those who trust in Him.

NAHUM 1:7 NLT

When peace like a river attendeth my way, when sorrow like sea-billows roll;
Whatever my lot, Thou hast taught me to say, "It is well, it is well with my soul."

HORATIO G. SPAFFORD

I have told you these things, so that in Me you may have peace. In this world you will have trouble. But take heart! I have overcome the world.

JOHN 16:33 NIV

Thro' many dangers, toils and snare,
I have already come. . . .

Thro' many dangers, toils and snare,
I have already come. . . .

The sufferings we encounter in life...are meant to help us partake of Christ.... God strips us of our "self-help" mind-set. We are forced to our knees and driven to lean on His grace. Then...can God impart His Son's character to us.

JONI EARECKSON TADA

Don't run from suffering; embrace it. Follow Me and I'll show you how. Self-help is no help at all. Self-sacrifice is the way, My way, to finding yourself, your true self.

MATTHEW 16:25 THE MESSAGE

Thro' many dangers,
toils and snare,
I have already come;
'Tis grace has brought me
safe thus far,
And grace will
lead me home.

'Tis grace has brought me safe thus far,
And grace will lead me home....

There is no rest in the heart of God until He knows that we are at rest in His grace.

LLOYD JOHN OGILVIE

The Lord longs to be gracious to you; He rises to show you compassion. For the Lord is a God of justice. Blessed are all who wait for Him!

ISAIAH 30:18 NIV

If the Lord be with us, we have no cause of fear. His eye is upon us, His arm over us, His ear open to our prayer— His grace sufficient, His promise unchangeable.

JOHN NEWTON

I am the Lord your God, who holds your right hand, and I tell you, "Don't be afraid. I will help you."

ISAIAH 41:13 NCV

'Tis grace has brought me safe thus far,
And grace will lead me home. . . .

'Tis grace has brought me safe thus far,
And grace will lead me home. . . .

Grace is but glory begun and glory is but grace perfected.

JONATHAN EDWARDS

*Keep a firm grip on the faith. The suffering won't last forever.
It won't be long before this generous God who has great plans
for us in Christ—eternal and glorious plans they are!—will
have you...on your feet for good.*

1 PETER 5:10-11 THE MESSAGE

*D*o not take over much thought for tomorrow. God, who has led you safely on so far, will lead you on to the end. Be altogether at rest in the loving holy confidence which you ought to have in His heavenly Providence.

FRANCIS DE SALES

The peace of God, which surpasses all understanding, will guard your hearts and minds through Christ Jesus.

PHILIPPIANS 4:7 NKJV

'Tis grace has brought me safe thus far,
And grace will lead me home. . . .

'Tis grace has brought me safe thus far,
And grace will lead me home....

························

························

························

························

························

························

························

························

························

························

Grace is love that cares and stoops and rescues.

JOHN R. W. STOTT

This is how God showed His love for us: God sent His only Son into the world so we might live through Him.

1 JOHN 4:10 THE MESSAGE

God never abandons anyone on whom He has set His love; nor does Christ, the good shepherd, ever lose track of His sheep.

J. I. PACKER

I am the good shepherd. The good shepherd gives His life for the sheep.

JOHN 10:11 NKJV

'Tis grace has brought me safe thus far,
And grace will lead me home....

'Tis grace has brought me safe thus far,
And grace will lead me home. . . .

Living a life of faith means never knowing where you are being led. But it does mean loving and knowing the One who is leading. It is literally a life of faith... a life of knowing Him who calls us to go.

OSWALD CHAMBERS

Know that the Lord your God is God, the faithful God. He will keep His agreement of love for a thousand lifetimes for people who love Him and obey His commands.

DEUTERONOMY 7:9 NCV

The Lord has promised
good to me.
His word my hope secures;
He will my shield
and portion be,
As long as life endures.

The Lord has promised good to me.
His Word my hope secures. . . .

*H*ave you ever thought that in every action of grace in
your heart you have the whole omnipotence
of God engaged to bless you?

ANDREW MURRAY

*N*ow I am putting you in the care of God and the message
about His grace. It is able to give you strength, and it will give
you the blessings God has for all His holy people.

ACTS 20:32 NCV

Forgiveness is not acting as if things are just the same as before the offense.... Things will never be the same. By the grace of God they can be a thousand times better, but they will never again be the same.

RICHARD J. FOSTER

If anyone belongs to Christ, there is a new creation. The old things have gone; everything is made new!

2 CORINTHIANS 5:17 NCV

The Lord has promised good to me.
His Word my hope secures....

The Lord has promised good to me.
His Word my hope secures. . . .

The conversion from mistrust to trust is a confident
quest seeking the spiritual meaning of human existence.
Grace abounds and walks around the edges of our
everyday experience.

BRENNAN MANNING

God makes everything come out right.... God is sheer mercy
and grace; not easily angered, He's rich in love.

PSALM 103:6, 8 THE MESSAGE

God makes a promise—faith believes it, hope anticipates it, patience quietly awaits it.

But we have the true hope that comes from being made right with God, and by the Spirit we wait eagerly for this hope.

GALATIANS 5:5 NCV

The Lord has promised good to me.
His Word my hope secures. . . .

The Lord has promised good to me.
His Word my hope secures. . . .

We must drink deeply from the very Source the deep calm and peace of interior quietude and refreshment of God, allowing the pure water of divine grace to flow plentifully and unceasingly from the Source itself.

MOTHER TERESA

For He satisfies the thirsty and fills the hungry with good things.

PSALM 107:9 NLT

*D*o you believe that God is near? He wants you to. He wants you to know that He is in the midst of your world. Wherever you are as you read these words, He is present.... He's near. And He is more than near. He is active.

MAX LUCADO

I am with you, and I will protect you wherever you go. One day I will bring you back to this land. I will not leave you until I have finished giving you everything I have promised you.

GENESIS 28:15 NLT

The Lord has promised good to me.
His Word my hope secures. . . .

The Lord has promised good to me.
His Word my hope secures. . . .

....

....

....

....

....

....

....

....

....

....

....

*Commit to hope. There's reason to! For the believer, hope
is divinely assured things that aren't here yet! Our hope is
grounded in unshakable promises.*

JACK HAYFORD

*You have this faith and love because of your hope, and what
you hope for is kept safe for you in heaven. You learned about
this hope when you heard the message about the truth,
the Good News.*

COLOSSIANS 1:5 NCV

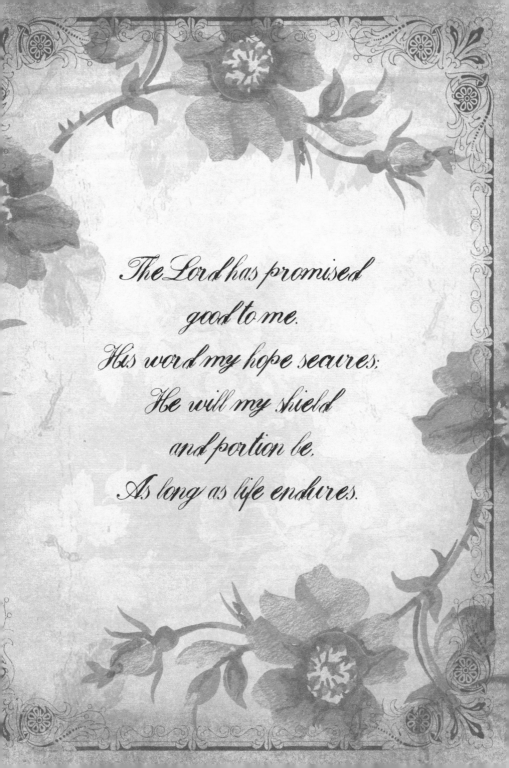

The Lord has promised
good to me.
His word my hope secures;
He will my shield
and portion be.
As long as life endures.

He will my shield and portion be,
As long as life endures....

Incredible as it may seem, God wants our companionship. He wants to have us close to Him. He wants to be a father to us, to shield us, to protect us, to counsel us, and to guide us in our way through life.

BILLY GRAHAM

May you be filled with joy, always thanking the Father. He has enabled you to share in the inheritance that belongs to His people, who live in the light.

COLOSSIANS 1:11-12 NLT

Faith is a living, daring confidence in God's grace, so sure and certain that a man could stake his life on it a thousand times.

MARTIN LUTHER

Take up the shield of faith, with which you can extinguish all the flaming arrows of the evil one.

EPHESIANS 6:16 NIV

He will my shield and portion be.
As long as life endures....

He will my shield and portion be,
As long as life endures....

Grace...like the Lord, the giver, never fails from age to age.

JOHN NEWTON

May our Lord...encourage you and strengthen you in every good thing you do and say. God loved us, and through His grace He gave us a good hope and encouragement that continues forever.

2 THESSALONIANS 2:16 NCV

Grasp the fact that God is for you...and you will find in thus knowing God as your sovereign protector, irrevocably committed to you in the covenant of grace, both freedom from fear and new strength for the fight.

J. I. PACKER

The Lord is a shelter for the oppressed, a refuge in times of trouble.

PSALM 9:9 NLT

He will my shield and portion be,
As long as life endures. . . .

He will my shield and portion be,
As long as life endures....

Lord, I freely yield all my freedom to You.... You have given me anything I am or have; I give it all back to You to stand under Your will alone. Your love and Your grace are enough for me; I shall ask for nothing more.

"My grace is sufficient for you, for My strength is made perfect in weakness." Therefore most gladly I will rather boast in my infirmities, that the power of Christ may rest upon me.

2 CORINTHIANS 12:9 NKJV

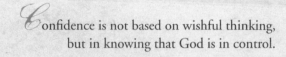

*Confidence is not based on wishful thinking,
but in knowing that God is in control.*

*I am still confident of this: I will see the goodness of the Lord
in the land of the living.*

PSALM 27:13 NIV

He will my shield and portion be,
As long as life endures....

He will my shield and portion be,
As long as life endures. . . .

*L*et your faith in Christ...be in the quiet confidence that
He will...every moment keep you as the apple of His eye,
keep you in perfect peace and in the sure experience of all
the light and the strength you need in His service.

ANDREW MURRAY

*K*eep me as the apple of Your eye; hide me under the shadow
of Your wings.

PSALM 17:8 NKJV

Yes, when this flesh
and heart shall fail,
And mortal life shall cease;
I shall profess,
within the vail,
A life of joy and peace.

I shall profess, within the vail,
A life of joy and peace....

*G*race is...an outpouring, a boundless offering of God's self to us, suffering with us, overflowing with tenderness. Grace is God's passion.

GERALD G. MAY

*T*he amazing grace of the Master, Jesus Christ, the extravagant love of God, the intimate friendship of the Holy Spirit, be with all of you.

2 CORINTHIANS 13:14 THE MESSAGE

To be grateful is to recognize the Love of God in everything He has given us—and He has given us everything. Every breath we draw is a gift of His love, every moment of existence is a gift of grace.

THOMAS MERTON

The God who made the world and everything in it is the Lord of heaven and earth.... He Himself gives all men life and breath and everything else.

ACTS 17:24-25 NIV

I shall profess, within the vail,
A life of joy and peace. . . .

I shall profess, within the vail,
A life of joy and peace. . . .

For it is through the living witness of others that we are drawn to God at all. It is because of His creatures, and His work in them, that we come to praise Him.

TERESA OF AVILA

In everything we have done in the world...we have had an honest and sincere heart from God. We did this by God's grace.

2 CORINTHIANS 1:12 NCV

Grace tells us that we are accepted just as we are. We may not be the kind of people we want to be,...we may have more failures than achievements,...we may not even be happy, but we are nonetheless accepted by God, held in His hands.

McCULLOUGH

We throw open our doors to God and discover at the same moment that He has already thrown open His door to us. We find ourselves standing where we always hoped we might stand—out in the wide open spaces of God's grace and glory.

ROMANS 5:2 THE MESSAGE

I shall profess, within the vail,
A life of joy and peace....

I shall profess, within the vail,
A life of joy and peace....

There is nothing but God's grace. We walk upon it; we breathe it; we live and die by it; it makes the nails and axles of the universe.

ROBERT LOUIS STEVENSON

"By His power we live and move and exist." Some of your own poets have said: "For we are His children."

ACTS 17:28 NCV

God's children who joyously know and claim who they are and whose they are, will be most likely to manifest the family likeness, just because they know they are His children.

ALICE CHAPIN

For you are all sons of God through faith in Christ Jesus.

GALATIANS 3:26 NKJV

I shall profess, within the vail,
A life of joy and peace....

I shall profess, within the vail,
A life of joy and peace....

The hope we have in Christ is an absolute certainty.
We can be sure that the place Christ is preparing for us will
be ready when we arrive, because with Him nothing is left
to chance. Everything He promised He will deliver.

BILLY GRAHAM

*Lord God, you are God, and your words are true. And you
have promised these good things to me.*

2 SAMUEL 7:28 NCV

Yes, when this flesh
and heart shall fail,
And mortal life shall cease;
I shall profess,
within the vail,
A life of joy and peace.

I shall profess, within the vail,
A life of joy and peace. . . .

········

········

········

········

········

········

········

········

········

$\mathcal{O}$ur hearts were made to enjoy the One who created them. Too deeply planted to be much affected by the ups and downs of life, this joy is a knowing and a being known by our Creator. He sets our hearts alight with radiant joy.

$\mathcal{I}$ have come that they may have life, and that they may have it more abundantly.

JOHN 10:10 NKJV

All those who live with any degree of serenity
live by some assurance of grace.

REINHOLD NEIBUHR

Be strong and take heart, all you who hope in the Lord.
PSALM 31:24 NIV

I shall profess, within the vail,
A life of joy and peace. . . .

I shall profess, within the vail,
A life of joy and peace. . . .

The purpose of grace is primarily to restore our relationship with God.... The work of grace aims at... an ever deeper knowledge of God, and an ever closer fellowship with Him. Grace is God drawing us to Himself.

J. I. PACKER

The Lord is good to those who hope in Him, to those who seek Him.

LAMENTATIONS 3:25 NCV

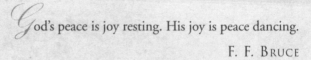

God's peace is joy resting. His joy is peace dancing.

F. F. BRUCE

You will go out in joy and be led forth in peace;
the mountains and hills will burst into song before you,
and all the trees of the field will clap their hands.

ISAIAH 55:12 NIV

I shall profess, within the vail,
A life of joy and peace. . . .

I shall profess, within the vail,
A life of joy and peace. . . .

Love comes while we rest against our Father's chest.
Joy comes when we catch the rhythms of His heart.
Peace comes when we live in harmony with those rhythms.

KEN GIRE

And because we are His children, God has sent the Spirit of
His Son into our hearts, prompting us to call out,
"Abba, Father."

GALATIANS 4:6 NLT

As we grow in our capacities to see and enjoy the joys that God has placed in our lives, life becomes a glorious experience of discovering His endless wonders.

I will greatly rejoice in the Lord, my soul shall be joyful in my God.

ISAIAH 61:10 NKJV

I shall profess, within the vail,
A life of joy and peace. . . .

I shall profess, within the vail,
A life of joy and peace. . . .

_It_ is God's knowledge of me, His careful husbanding of the ground of my being, His constant presence in the garden of my little life that guarantees my joy.

W. PHILLIP KELLER

Now to Him who is able to keep you from stumbling, and to present you faultless before the presence of His glory with exceeding joy, to God our Savior, Who alone is wise, be glory and majesty, dominion and power, both now and forever. Amen.

JUDE 1:24-25 NKJV

The earth shall soon
dissolve like snow,
The sun forbear to shine;
But God, who called
me here below,
Will be for ever mine.

But God, who called me here below,
Will be for ever mine....

The secret of life is that all we have and are
is a gift of grace to be shared.

LLOYD JOHN OGILVIE

*God, mark us with grace and blessing! Smile! The whole
country will see how You work.... God! Let people
thank and enjoy You.*

PSALM 67:1-2 THE MESSAGE

*T*he place where God calls you to is the place where your deep gladness and the world's deep hunger meet.

FREDERICK BUECHNER

I, the Lord, have called you to demonstrate My righteousness.
I will take you by the hand and guard you.

ISAIAH 42:6 NLT

But God, who called me here below,
Will be for ever mine. . . .

But God, who called me here below,
Will be for ever mine....

Whatever the circumstances, whatever the call, whatever the duty, whatever the price, whatever the sacrifice—His strength will be your strength in your hour of need.

BILLY GRAHAM

The spacious, free life is from God, it's also protected and safe. God-strengthened, we're delivered from evil—when we run to Him, He saves us.

PSALM 37:39 THE MESSAGE

That is God's call to us—simply to be people who are content to live close to Him and to renew the kind of life in which the closeness is felt and experienced.

THOMAS MERTON

You're blessed when you're content with just who you are— no more, no less. That's the moment you find yourselves proud owners of everything that can't be bought.

MATTHEW 5:5 THE MESSAGE

But God, who called me here below,
Will be for ever mine....

But God, who called me here below,
Will be for ever mine....

....

....

....

....

....

....

....

....

....

....

*ℛecognizing who we are in Christ and aligning our life
with God's purpose for us gives a sense of destiny....
It gives form and direction to our life.*

JEAN FLEMING

*Whether you turn to the right or to the left, your ears will
hear a voice behind you, saying, "This is the way; walk in it."*

ISAIAH 30:21 NIV

Have a purpose in life, and having it, throw into your
work such strength of mind and muscle
as God has given you.

THOMAS CARLYLE

*I still belong to You; You hold my right hand. You guide me
with Your counsel, leading me to a glorious destiny.*

PSALM 73:23-24 NLT

But God, who called me here below,
Will be for ever mine. . . .

But God, who called me here below,
Will be for ever mine....

....

....

....

....

....

....

....

....

....

....

It is my calling to treat every human being with grace and dignity, to treat every person, whether encountered in a palace or a gas station, as a life made in the image of God.

SHEILA WALSH

Dear friends, we should love each other, because love comes from God. Everyone who loves has become God's child and knows God. Whoever does not love does not know God, because God is love.

1 JOHN 4:7-8 NCV

The earth shall soon
dissolve like snow,
The sun forbear to shine;
But God, who called
me here below,
Will be for ever mine.

But God, who called me here below,
Will be for ever mine. . . .

Eternity is at our hearts, pressing upon our time-torn lives, warming us...calling us home unto Itself. Yielding to these persuasions...utterly and completely, to the Light within, is the beginning of true life.

THOMAS R. KELLY

Yet God has made everything beautiful for its own time. He has planted eternity in the human heart, but even so, people cannot see the whole scope of God's work from beginning to end.

ECCLESIASTES 3:11 NLT

We have been given the breath of life, designed with a unique, one-of-a-kind soul that exists forever—whether we live it as a burden or a joy or with indifference doesn't change the fact that we've been given the gift of *being* now and forever.

You have made known to me the path of life;
You will fill me with joy in Your presence,
with eternal pleasures at Your right hand.

PSALM 16:11 NIV

But God, who called me here below,
Will be for ever mine. . . .

But God, who called me here below,
Will be for ever mine. . . .

....

....

....

....

....

....

....

....

....

....

*Every action of our lives touches a chord that
vibrates in Eternity.*

EDWIN HUBBEL CHAPIN

*You can be sure that God will take care of everything you
need, His generosity exceeding even yours in the glory that
pours from Jesus. Our God and Father abounds in glory
that just pours out into eternity.*

PHILIPPIANS 4:18 THE MESSAGE

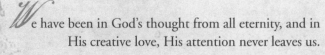

We have been in God's thought from all eternity, and in
His creative love, His attention never leaves us.

MICHAEL QUOIST

From eternity to eternity I am God. No one can snatch anyone
out of My hand. No one can undo what I have done.

ISAIAH 43:13 NLT

But God, who called me here below,
Will be for ever mine....

But God, who called me here below,
Will be for ever mine. . . .

....

....

....

....

....

....

....

....

....

....

Let Jesus be in your heart, eternity in your spirit, the
world under your feet, the will of God in your actions.
And let the love of God shine forth from you.

CATHERINE OF GENOA

My dear children, let's not just talk about love;
let's practice real love. This is the only way we'll know
we're living truly, living in God's reality.

1 JOHN 3:18 THE MESSAGE

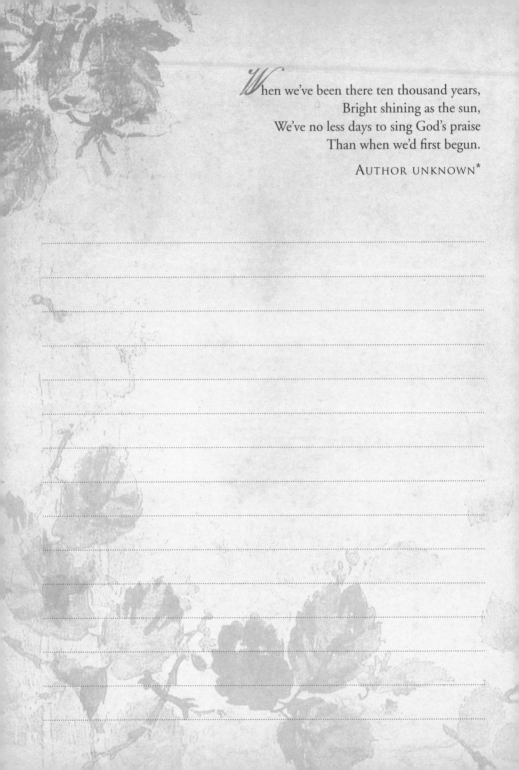

When we've been there ten thousand years,
Bright shining as the sun,
We've no less days to sing God's praise
Than when we'd first begun.

AUTHOR UNKNOWN*

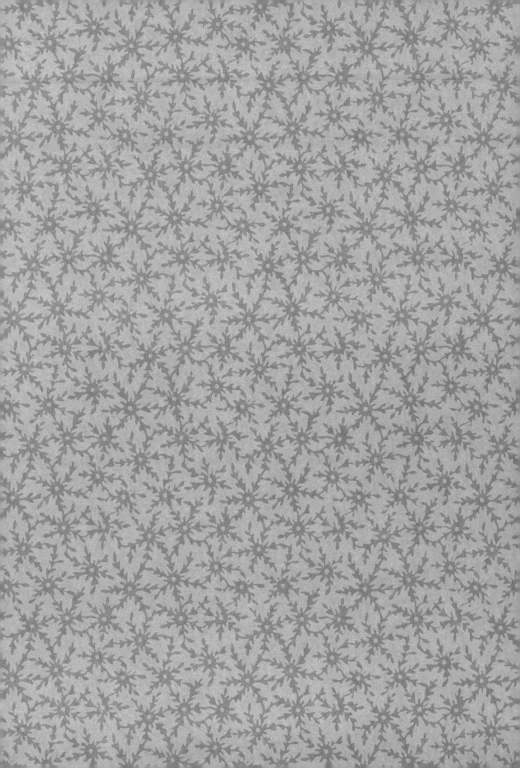

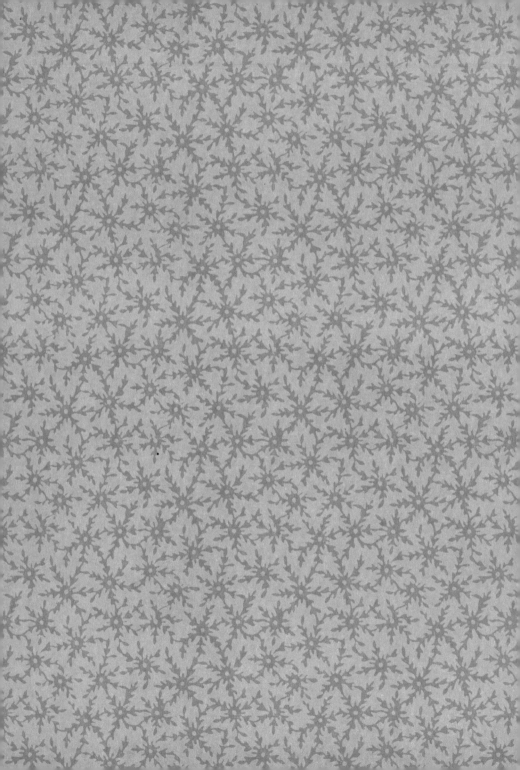